Live On

Live On

Inspirational Poems & Quotes

Vanessa A. Jackson Austin

Bloomington, IN  Milton Keynes, UK

authorHOUSE™

AuthorHouse™
1663 Liberty Drive, Suite 200
Bloomington, IN 47403
www.authorhouse.com
Phone: 1-800-839-8640

AuthorHouse™ UK Ltd.
500 Avebury Boulevard
Central Milton Keynes, MK9 2BE
www.authorhouse.co.uk
Phone: 08001974150

First published by AuthorHouse 6/9/2006

ISBN: 1-4259-3240-1 (sc)

Printed in the United States of America
Bloomington, Indiana

This book is printed on acid-free paper.

Cover art by Cedric J. Austin

In loving memory of my mother,
Elzater L. Hogue Jackson
And my brother, Glennford L. Jackson...
Both of whom visit me from time to time in my dreams.

Dedication and Acknowledgements

This book is dedicated to my kind and loving husband and friend, Frederick, and to our sons, Cedric, Andre,' and Brian. Hold onto these scriptures, "When you pass through the waters, I (God) will be with you. When you cross rivers, you will not drown. When you walk through fire, you will not be burned, nor will the flames hurt you." *Isaiah 43:2 (NCV)* and "Always remember what is written in the Book of the Teachings. Study it day and night to be sure to obey everything that is written there. If you do this, you will be wise and successful in everything." *Joshua 1:8 (NCV)*

I thank my family members and friends, because you all know I have had my poetry and quotes written for the good part of three years. There have been trials and a seemingly uphill battle, as I have worked tirelessly to accomplish this goal. And now God has blessed us to see this time through—where the publication of my first book has become a reality. Therefore, I thank each of you for your support and genuineness.

I am especially grateful to my son, Cedric, my cross country runner, and true to heart basketball player, for your artistic design on the front and back cover of *"Live On;" CABBIT Designs (Cedric Andre' Brian Branded It).* I also would like to thank Buddie C. Jackson, my dad, for your love and continued support in my endeavors.

How happy and excited I am to have located the editor of my book. She is God sent, no doubt. Thank you, Dedra L.

Muhammad for diligently working with me as you proofread my material. God Bless you!

Above all, I give honor, praise, and glory to Almighty God, who has given me **all** of the words to my Christian poetry and quotes. Without you, God, I would not have written and published this book.

CONTENTS

Poems

Beginning Scripture..*xi*

Hold On.. 1

How I Know Him 2

Now is the Time 3

Hanging by a Thread 4

God I Trust You 5

My Prayer 6

Find Him.. 7

What a Creation 8

He is Real 9

Hard Times 10

In Control 11

In Remembrance of You..12

I Remember..13

Our Wedding Prayer..14

Time After Time 15

Clutter, Clutter, Clutter 16

No End 17

Help Me, Lord 18

Never Forgotten 19

Live the Right Way 21

Are You Prepared 22

My Wake Up Call 23

Live On...24

Small Quotes for Big Hearts

Week One..28

Week Two..29

Week Three 30

Week Four 31

Ending Scripture...*33*

*"Trust the Lord with all your heart, and don't depend on your understanding. Remember the Lord in all you do, and he will give you success." *Proverbs 3:5-6 (NCV)*

*Taken from New Century Version (NCV)

Hold On

Hold on my child, for I am on the way,
Don't despair, not even for a day.

For this storm may seem too hard to bear,
But don't forget, I do care.

I have told you that weeping may endure for a night,
But joy comes in the morning light.

Hold on, for I will never leave you,
Because my promises are forever true.

Whenever you feel low and burdened,
Call upon Almighty God, my humble servants.

You can find me at your lowest points,
The Everlasting Father most surely annoints.

Related Scriptures:

Jeremiah 32:27
Isaiah 43:2
Isaiah 59:1
Psalm 30:5
2 Corinthians 1:3-11
2 Corinthians 4:8-10&17

How I Know Him

How can I begín to tell you
What God has done for me?
He has been my companion
When the way has been hard to see.

When my journey has been treacherous and far,
God has been my shining star.
This is how I know Him.

He has guided me through many storms,
Through times when I have found it
Troubling to carry on.

He has directed me, protected me,
Never neglected me,
Without the Lord, I can't imagine
Where I would be.

Related Scriptures:

Joshua 1:8
Isaiah 58:11
Psalm 25:9
Psalm 32:8
Proverbs 32:5-6

Now is the Time

Now is the time to live right,
For God is coming like a thief in the night.

Now is the time to pray without ceasing,
For learning God's word is quite easy.

Now is the time to study God's word more,
For he is steadily knocking at your door.

Now is the time to seek the Lord, while he can still be found,
For this golden opportunity won't always be around.

Now is the time to invite Christ into your heart,
For He wants to be your main part.

Now is the time to get your house in order,
For the time of Christ's imminent return is getting shorter & shorter.

Now is the time to get in sync,
Because it is later than you think.

Related Scriptures:

Isaiah 55:6-7
Psalm 119:160
Matthew 24:43-44
Luke 12:35-40
2 Peter 3:10
Revelation 3:3

Hanging by a Thread

When life's awkward situations
Have come my way,
I don't lose heart and go astray.

When I have been down to my last dime,
That is just when the Lord steps in;
He's always right on time.

Even when I have gone down the wrong path in life,
God reminds me;
The strength of growing is to endure strife.

When I feel overwhelmed in this life;
When I'm hanging by a thread,
I ask God to be my guide and by Him I am led.

Related Scriptures:

Deuteronomy 31:6
Psalm 48:14
Psalm 121:1-8
Hebrews 13:5
1 Peter 5:7

God I Trust You

As I sleep at night,
My soul You keep with all Your Might,
Therefore,
God I trust you.

When times get too hard to bear,
I turn to You who Cares,
Because
God I trust you.

When my bills are due,
Not knowing what to do,
Yet still...
God I trust you.

When my friends grow small and few,
I know I have You,
And that's why
God I trust you.

When the enemy tries to take control,
I know to whom I must go,
God I will always
Trust you.

Related Scriptures:

Isaiah 26:3-4
Psalm 27:1
Psalm 37:5
Psalm 56:3
Psalm 62:7-8
Psalm 91:2
Psalm 118:8
Proverbs 30:5

My Prayer

God, Almighty Father
I need your help today,
I need your love and guidance
In a mighty, mighty way.

At times I get confused and
I don't understand,
Your plans
For my life, so please take my hand.

You are in control,
And know
The way I am to go.
Heavenly Father, I am asking for
Discernment in
Recognizing within,
The things I need to know
And
The way I am to go.

Related Scriptures:

Psalm 55:17
Jeremiah 29:11
Matthew 6:6-8
Philippians 4:6
1 Thessalonians 5:17
James 5:16
1 Peter 3:12

Find Him

When I find myself in a tight fix,
I often get lost in the crowd, refusing to mingle and mix.

That is when I talk to the Lord,
The Prince of Peace, Almighty God.

He knows just how I feel,
Almighty God would never, ever squeal.

When I am especially lonely and afraid,
The Lord gives me His ever glorious shade.

Why not find out how great God's love is:
Geniune, and coming from heaven above is

What His love
Is.

Related Scriptures:

Psalm 34:4
Psalm 105:4
Proverbs 8:17
Jeremiah 29:13
Lamentations 3:25

What a Creation

God's creations are all around,
From heaven above, to the bottom of the ground.

Look at the deep blue sea,
Oh!
How her bountifulness truly amazes me.

As I watch the stars in the sky,
They appear to follow me as I pass by.

The flowers have such beautiful colors,
Their smells give such a sweet aroma.

The clouds in the sky seem so soft and white,
Just watching each one is such a magnificient sight.

How the birds in the air sing such lovely songs,
Their sounds remind me of the church bells as they ring,
"Ding-dong".

Trees of every kind stand so tall,
Just notice how each one drops their leaves in the
midst of fall.

What a sight to see: God's wonderful creation,
For His love crosses each and every generation.

Related Scriptures:

Genesis 1:1-31
Psalm 136:5-9
John 1:3

He is Real

Things may be bleak right now,
But God knows how,
As you fall on your knees and bow,
He's real.

You may be in doubt,
But He will never leave you without,
He's real.

Situations in your life might have you upset,
But never forget,
He's real.

When life gives you a raw deal,
Try God, for He never will,
He's real.

When you are drained from life's stress and strain,
God's love is off the chain,
He's real.

Just when you are about to give up,
In God you can trust,
For He is real.

Related Scriptures:

Psalm 145:14-16
Luke 1:37
Luke 12:28
John 6:37-38
Philippians 4:19

Hard Times

Hard times come and they go,
In order for us to draw closer to God,
That we might grow.

For if we never faced hard times,
We would think the sun is always
Supposed to shine.

Without hard times, how would we know
That God is here for us,
Especially when we are low?

Hard times can make us or break us,
That is why we should turn to God,
The one and only to trust.

Related Scriptures:

Joshua 1:5
Micah 7:7-8
Psalm 34:19&22
Psalm 119:71
James 4:8

In Control

I am
In control of this train,
And while you ride,
There is much to gain.

I am
Alpha and Omega,
The beginning and the end.
Without me, you will never, ever win.

Come to me all who are heavy laden
Gentle lads and fair maidens
I will give you rest,
After you pass the submissive test.

I will make you the best of the best
For I recall when you went through the fiery furnace,
You looked for me:
Dependable, honest, and earnest.

So when you are feeling down and blue,
I am in control
And I will help you.

Related Scriptures:

Proverbs 21:1
Matthew 11:28-30
1 Peter 5:7
Revelation 1:8
Revelation 22:13

In Remembrance of You

Mother, I recall the good times we had,
And how you would bring laughter and
Joy to those who were sad.

You were the kind of person
Who was full of sparkle and fun,
And you never ceased to have time for anyone.

But I know you had to go to your home on high,
To be with God's Almighty
Paradise in the sky.

Mother, my love for you is undying,
For life down here without you
Has been trying.

But with God on my side and your love
Engraved in my heart,
This special day I long for you, As I begin a new start.

Mother, I know that with God is where you must be,
Because I feel your presence in my Heart
Smiling down on me.

Related Scriptures:

Psalm 128:3
Proverbs 31:10-15&25-31
Ephesians 6:1-3

I Remember

I remember having you as a brother,
Was like having no other.
You were always full of laughter and fun,
Your smile as bright as the rays of the sun.
I remember when seeing you was always a joy,
You had a helping hand for anyone.
Giving to others you had no end,
No wonder you had many acquaintances and friends.

I remember when you told me about life,
And how excited you were when I became a wife.
But when you lost your job and didn't know what to do,
I recall how difficult it was for you and your family, too.
When another location you accepted,
How I felt in my heart it was wrong,
But I had to accept your decisión and try to be strong.

You were in my heart as you traveled that lonely
highway,
For I know God protected you each and every day.
And when the time came for you to go away,
God already knew you couldn't stay.
There is no doubt, heaven is your home,
But I do miss you since you've been gone.
But I will always remember your sunshine and joy,
And the goodness in your heart you had for everyone.

Related Scriptures:

Genesis 13:8
Genesis 14:14
Mark 3:33-35
Luke 15:27&32

Our Wedding Prayer

We thank you Lord for this joyous day,
For our lives and for bringing us this way.

For our families and for our friends,
Who have come to rejoice in our new beginning.

Heavenly Father you have brought us both together
and
Our prayer is for you to bless us forever and forever.

Amen

Related Scriptures:

Matthew 19:5-6
1 Corinthians 7:10-17
2 Corinthians 6:14-17
Ephesians 5:21-33
Hebrews 13:4

Time After Time

Time after time when I have cried,
I remember on the cross
You hung your head and died.

Time after time when I have gone astray,
Your Omnipotent Presence let me know
You are the way.

Time after time
You have come to my rescue,
When I was lonely and didn't know what to do.

Time after time, Lord I have fallen down,
Still, when I turned to you, you lifted me off the ground
Turned my whole life around.

Time after time, Oh Lord,
You have given me hope,
Just when I have thrown up my hands and said nope.

Related Scriptures:

Joshua 1:9
Psalm 31:24
Psalm 118:5
John 14:6
Romans 5:5
1 Peter 3:15

Clutter, Clutter, Clutter

Clutter, Clutter I have so much clutter,
I feel as though my life is in the gutter.

I know God does not want me this way,
For He told me to always pray.

For insight into my life,
And to always walk aright.

So, God please help me right now,
Because without you, I don't know how.

Related Scriptures:

Ecclesiastes 7:29
Isaiah 65:24
Matthew 7:7-8
1 John 1:8-10

No End

There is no end to the miracles God can do,
He has been faithful to me and He can do the same for
you.

For God sent his son Jesús Christ to die on the cross,
And at the cross he paid for our sins at his cost.

In just a matter of time,
Jesús Christ turned water into wine.

With only five pieces of fish and two loaves of bread,
There were five thousand people whom Jesús fed.

Jesús also calmed the great storm at the sea,
And he protected the children of Israel from all of their
enemies.

And Jesús spent time giving sight to the blind,
All of these miracles he did with you and me in mind.

There is no end to the miracles God can do,
For He is the only one you can depend upon, too.

Related Scriptures:

Exodus 13:3&21-22
Exodus 14:13-14
Matthew 9:27-31
Matthew 14:15-21
Luke 13:11-13
John 2:1-11

Help Me, Lord

As I am comfronted with
The throes of life
Awkward situations all about,

The Devil trying to stir up doubt
I could throw up my hands,
And scream and shout.

Knowing that there are things I don't understand,
I pray: Almighty God, please
Take my hand.

Help me hold on when I am confused,
Remember me when I get torn apart,
Abused.

At times, I could hide in a cave,
When this world appears to be in a maze,
Got me all in a daze.

I say: Help me, Dear Lord
When I am breathless from this life I see,
Please hold me close
Care for me tenderly.

Related Scriptures:

Genesis 35:3
Isaiah 41:13
Psalm 40:1
Psalm 142:1-7

Never Forgotten

When God created the heavens and the earth,
He created Adam and Eve, too,

But eating from the tree of life,
Adam and Eve were forbidden to do.

By disobeying God's instructions, and eating from the
forbidden tree,
Their eyes were opened and they were able to see.

Never would man live in paradise again,
But God never forgot man, even when he sinned.

Though faced with heartaches and heartbreaks,
David, a man after God's own heart, came to grips
with his ongoing sins.

Joseph, being sold by his own brothers,
Continued to serve God, knowing, in Him there is no
other.

Abraham was told to sacrifice his son,
But God intervened and said, "The ram is the one."

Samson, whose strength was revealed in his hair, then
was deceived,
At the end, the Lord's power he received.

Peter, a disciple who wept after Jesús he denied,
Was forgiven after he acknowledged he had lied.

Job, a just and upright man who walked with God,
Endured much criticism and pain,
Continued to trust the Lord and in the end
He was restored and regained.

Jonah, a prophet who ran from God, was swallowed by
a huge fish,
Finally, obeyed God and in return God dismissed.

Daniel, a servant who refused to stop serving God,
Was thrown into the lion's den,
Yet he was rescued by God in the end.

Noah trusted God's instructions by building an ark,
And when the earth was flooded, Noah and his family
Prayed through the dark,
Trust in God they never forgot.

Moses, a man of God
Who had the power of God in the rod,
Led the children of Israel through the Red Sea,
Because God never forgot him, Moses believed.

Solomon, a man truly blessed with great wisdom and
wealth,
Learned at the end
That God's love he should never forget
For His love conquers all sins.

We should be like each servant;
They relied on and trusted God, which He never forgot,
For God loves each of us with all of His heart.

Related Scriptures:

Luke 17:5-6
2 Corinthians 5:7
2 Thessalonians 3:3
Hebrews 11:1-40

Live the Right Way

By living the right way,
We must always pray.

Asking God to be our Guide,
In his way we must abide.

For God's way is Eternal Life,
With God, we're purified by strife.

With prayer, guidance, and purification,
There's little room for wrong.

If we live the right way,
The heavenly Father will keep us safe and strong.

Related Scriptures:

Proverbs 10:12
Ephesians 4:17-24
Colossians 1:9-12
1 Thessalonians 4:1-12
1 Thessalonians 5:13-22
Hebrews 12:11-29
Hebrews 13:1-3&7-25

Are You Prepared

Are you prepared for that glorious day on high
When we will see our Master in the sky?

What a mighty day that will be,
Away from this tormenting world and at the
Saviour's feet.

So why set your treasures
Upon this earth?
For we are but dust and dirt.

Christ has said he will return,
Hence, aren't you looking for the crown
You have earned?

Are you prepared for that marvelous day?
For in obedience to Christ
Comes being shown the right way.

Related Scriptures:

Matthew 24:30-31
Luke 17:24-37
1 Corinthians 15:50-52
1 Thessalonians 4:14-18
1 Thessalonians 5:1-11
2 Peter 3:1-18
Revelation 22:6-7

My Wake Up Call

For my wake up call,
I feel as though I have endured it all.

For what God told me to do,
You can guess; I chose not to do.

But on the other hand, I must say,
By trusting in God He has truly made a way.

Through thick and thin, He came,
Just when I thought there was no one, I called His
name.

My heavenly Father is always there,
Just when I think He doesn't care.

Whenever I am in a bind,
I call upon the Lord, for He is always on time.

I will always remember my wake up call,
For God has let me know
He is faithful,
He is my all and all.

Related Scriptures:

Romans 7:14-24
Galatians 5:16-18

Live On

Live on my friend,
This and everyday.

For when fiery trials come your way,
Know that God is talking; He has the final say.

Trials come into our lives for good reasons,
And we must endure for all seasons.

Every season brings a change,
The changes may appear quite strange.

Still, you must live on
And stay with God,
For you are

Never alone.

Related Scriptures:

Psalm 40:2
Jeremiah 32:27
Romans 8:18
Hebrews 12:4-10
1 Peter 1:5-7
1 Peter 4:12-13

Small Quotes for Big Hearts

To those who might be down to the core. Know that with God's grace, He will supply us with much, much more.

Week One

Trust God with all of your heart, soul, and mind, and your problems will automatically be minimized.

Don't resent, be content.

The personal development of one's talents can be compared with searching for God's promises. One mustn't bury talents—instead, ask for His graceful help and as one step is taken in His direction, He will lead His servants in finding His purpose.

Life is like the flip of a coin; sometimes one is at the top and other times at the bottom, which bottom is merely a temporary position and preparation for up.

Week Two

God's promises are like hidden treasures waiting to be uncovered.

Jesus carries the burdens of the meek the same way in which he carried the cross.

Hardships in life can bring out the good; it can help you remember the things that you should.

One's abilities should never be underestimated, especially when it is understood that the Holy Spirit resides within and guides aright.

Week Three

Be joyful in life no matter how hard you are hit, for remember the" hit" represents the trial needed that might qualify one for a perfect fit.

Invest in prayer, for your returns are always guaranteed.

A steadfast attitude towards the challenges one must face will undoubtedly determine the outcome of the race.

Diversify your life: God's rainbows represent every color of us. Appreciate the purposefulness of all of His creatures.

Week Four

Everyday is wonderful, especially when God is placed at the center of one's activities.

By placing God first, and recognizing that He is the giver of talents, one can't go wrong, for it is through meekness and humility that all are made strong.

Even when we're at our wit's core, through His grace, might, and love, our cup runneth over forever more.

Need to build character?   God has a surplus supply with no hidden fees.

"I say this because I know what I am planning for you," says the Lord. I have good plans for you, not to hurt you. I will give you hope and a good future." *Jeremiah 29:11 (NCV)*

About the Author

Born in Gadsden, Alabama, I, Vanessa A. Jackson Austin, wrote poetry as a teenager, from experiences in my life. By the age of nineteen, publishing a book crossed my mind, but it never materialized. After receiving my high school diploma from Gadsden High School, I entered into college at Jacksonville State University, in which I graduated with a Bachelor of Science degree in Marketing, and a minor in Management. I also graduated from Athens State University with a Bachelor of Business Administration degree in Accounting. And years later, I graduated from Alabama A&M University with a Master's in Education in Business Education. I am an author/poet, bookkeeper, and jeweler maker. I also own and manage **Austin's Bookkeeping Service and CABBIT Designs** (Cedric Andre' Brian Branded It), all based in Harvest, Alabama, as well as where I presently reside. After working sixteen years with Redstone Arsenal, for the federal government, in various organizations, I was released from the last position. Although I rate my last position as a treacherous nightmare, I realize my imminent departure from that position was a disguised blessing, availing me the opportunity to reach others in a higher fashion. Thus, I am more accessible for His cause and purpose. God allowed my dependence on Him to increase in a way one can only understand through personal experience. And now I am here to tell others to **"Live On."** Let us refer to Psalms

46:1 and 7 (NCV) "God is our protection and our strength. He always helps in times of trouble. The Lord All-Powerful is with us; the God of Jacob is our defender." **Live On** is further dedicated *to those who might be down to the core. Know that with God's grace, He will supply us with much, much more.*